THIS JOURNAL BELONGS TO

_____

ISBN: 979-8-9861997-3-3

How To Read Tarot Cards

1. Relax and clear your mind, as this will allow you to hear your Intuition.

2. Clear your tarot deck to remove any stagnant energies that may hinder your reading (refer to next page).

3. Ask your question. This can be done either in your mind, or spoken out loud. If you do not have a specific question, you can simply ask the tarot cards "What do I need to know in this present moment?"

4. Cut the deck in half, placing the top half on the left. There should now be 2 piles of cards. Using the pile on the right, choose the top card and turn it over.

5. Reading your cards:

What is your first impression? Pay attention to your first feeling, thought, or reaction once you see the card.

Say the card's name out loud as this can sometimes open up pathways in the mind, thereby giving you new insights.

Pay attention to your body as your Intuition often communicates with you through physical feelings such as a fluttering stomach or tingling in your hands.

Look at every detail in the card. What is going on in the card? What colors are on the card? Does one color stand out more than another? What figures are in the card, whether human or animal? What symbols stand out to you from the card?

Deck Clearing Methods

The relationship you have with your cards will impact your ability to connect to and read your cards intuitively. There are a few ways to do this, so choose the one that resonates with you. You won't need to cleanse your deck before each reading, but you should cleanse a new deck, when someone else has handled your cards, or when readings aren't resonating with you.

1. Full Moon Clearing - Spread your deck out on a windowsill that has access to the moonlight. Leave them overnight, then collect them in the morning.

2. You can smudge sticks to clear the negative energies from your deck. Incense can also be used in the same way.

3. Meditate with your cards as this will help you connect to them. While meditating, visualize your cards being cleansed.

4. Use crystals to cleanse your deck. You can either place a healing crystal, such as clear quartz, on top of the deck while its it's not in use. Or you can place your cards into a bag/box with some healing crystals.

5. Set up a place that resonates with you, and say a prayer/blessing over your cards.

6. Shuffle your deck until the energy feels clear. It should feel like a weight has been lifted.

Tarot Tips

Take a moment to
ground yourself as
this will help with your
intuition.

Let go of expectations
and emotions as
much as possible.
Keep an open mind.

Take your time when
reading for yourself.
Information may come
slower than when reading
for someone else.

Focus more on the
traditional meaning of the
cards when reading for
yourself.

Pretend you're reading
for someone else. What
would you tell them?

YOU ARE

The Magick

BEHIND

The Tarot

Major Arcana

Pivotal Events

22 Cards

The Fool:	Beginnings. Adventure. Overconfidence
The Magician:	Study. Power. Concentration
The High Priestess:	Secrets. Intuition
The Empress:	Creation. New Projects. Fertility
The Emporer:	Assurance. Authority. Structure. Reason
The Heirophant:	Tradition. Knowledge
The Lovers:	Relationships. Union. Choices
The Chariot:	Victory. Action. Force
Strength:	Courage. Compassion
The Hermit:	Wisdom. Solitude. Introspection
The Wheel of Fortune:	Changes. Cycles
Justice:	Justice. Fairness. Harmony
The Hanged Man:	Relinquishing. Waiting. Sacrifice
Death:	Transformation
Temperance:	Trials. Challenges. Moderation
The Devil:	Deception. Resistance. Hidden Desires
The Tower:	Destruction. Catastrophe. Endings
The Star:	Hope. Revelation. Discovery
The Moon:	The Unknown. Illusion
The Sun:	Illumination. Happiness. Understanding
Judgement:	Acceptance. Adjustment. Reason
The World:	Completion. Fulfillment

Minor Arcana

Swords
Air, Reason

Ace (Potential)	Clarity
Two (Duality)	Decision
Three (Communication)	Sorrow
Four (Stability)	Rest
Five (Adversity)	Conflict
Six (Growth)	Transition
Seven (Faith)	Worries
Eight (Change)	Restrictions
Nine (Fruition)	Despair
Ten (Completion)	Defeat
Page (Messages)	Curiosity
Knight (Motion)	Restlessness
Queen (Influence)	Perceptive
King (Authority)	Inventive

Wands
Fire, Creativity

Ace (Potential)	New Energy	Eight (Change)	Change
Two (Duality)	Contemplation	Nine (Fruition)	Persistence
Three (Communication)	Exploration	Ten (Completion)	Burdens
Four (Stability)	Celebration	Page (Messages)	Discovery
Five (Adversity)	Disagreements	Knight (Motion)	Adventure
Six (Growth)	Success	Queen (Influence)	Strength
Seven (Faith)	Competition	King (Authority)	Visionary

Pentacles
Earth, Material

Ace (Potential)	Prosperity
Two (Duality)	Balance
Three (Communication)	Teamwork
Four (Stability)	Stability
Five (Adversity)	Worry
Six (Growth)	Generosity
Seven (Faith)	Profit
Eight (Change)	Hard Work
Nine (Fruition)	Refinement
Ten (Completion)	Satisfaction
Page (Messages)	New Enterprise
Knight (Motion)	Efficiency
Queen (Influence)	Down-to-earth
King (Authority)	Responsibility

Cups
Water, Emotion

Ace (Potential)	Compassion	Eight (Change)	Escapism
Two (Duality)	Love	Nine (Fruition)	Satisfaction
Three (Communication)	Friendship	Ten (Completion)	Happiness
Four (Stability)	Contemplation	Page (Messages)	Creativity
Five (Adversity)	Grief	Knight (Motion)	Romantic
Six (Growth)	Innocence	Queen (Influence)	Compassionate
Seven (Faith)	Illusion	King (Authority)	Emotional Balance

Animal Symbols

~ Tarot Meanings ~

 Bull - Determination, Beauty, Indulgence, Sexuality

 Lion - Honor, Strength, Mastery

 Cat - Mystery, Psychic Ability, Intuition

 Lizard - Fire Element, Heat

 Crayfish - Emotions, Rivers, Females

 Rabbit - Good Luck, Fertility, Sexuality

 Dog - Friendship, **Confidantes, Followers**

 Snake - **Temptation, Choices, Sex**

 Fish - Water, Emotions, Feelings

 Tortoise - Wisdom, Experts, **Achievements**

 Horse - Initiative, Hard Work, **Friends**

 Wolf - Intuition, Nature

Mythological Creatures

~Tarot Meanings~

The Typhoon found on the Wheel of Fortune means that your fortune is turning. If you're already experiencing a negative streak, then things may be changing for the better. If you're having a positive streak, you should prepare for some negative downturns. The outcome may depend on whether your reading was of a positive or negative nature.

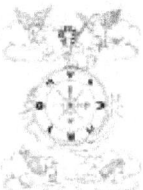

The Tetramorph can be found on The Wheel of Fortune, and The World cards. The different heads are meant to represent the 4 authors of the 4 Evangelists: Luke as the ox, John as the Eagle, Mark as the lion, and Matthew as the man. They can also be representative of astrological signs: Taurus, Leo, Scorpio, and Aquarius.

The Sphinx can be found on The Wheel of Fortune, and The Chariot cards. There are different interpretations of its meaning however, so consider all of the elements that are popping out to you from the cards. One meaning is that the white sphinx symbolizes mercy, while the black sphinx is representative of severity. Another interpretation is that of divine right and nobility.

The Dragon can be found on The 7 of Cups. Dragons symbolize protection, prosperity, wisdom, and magic. Dragons are the guardian of the treasures, and the hidden potential that lies within your subconscious mind.

The Chimera can be found on The 2 of Cups. In Greek mythology, the chimera is a creature of cunning and strength. It is also depicted as being female; therefore, representing the mystic connection with wild feminine energy. Other interpretations are that of temptation, as well as the male and female aspects of love.

Color Meanings

Black: **Transformation, Endings,
Protection**

Blue: **Communication, Subconscious**

Brown: **Earth Connection, Grounded**

Green: **Prosperity, Abundance,
Growth**

Orange: **Creativity, Fun, Playful**

Purple: **Spirituality, Intuition,
Prestige**

Red: **Passion, Confidence,
Power**

White: **Purity, Innocence, Mysticism**

Yellow: **Strength, Positivity,
Conciousness**

Numerology

1. New Beginnings, Opportunity, Potential

2. Balance, Choices, Duality

3. Expression, Groups, Growth, Relationships

4. Foundations, Planning, Stability

5. Change, Conflict, Rebuilding

6. Compassion, Harmony, Problem-Solving, Success

7. Faith, Reflection, Wisdom

8. Action, Change, Movement

9. Attainment, Fruition, Fulfillment

10. Completion, End-of-Cycle, Renewal, Transformation

Archangel & Planetary Correspondence

Card:	Archangels:	Planet:
The Chariot	Camael, Gabriel	Cancer
Death	Azrael, Camael	Scorpio
The Devil	Cassiel, Michael	Capricorn
The Emporer	Camael, Nathaniel	Aries
The Empress	Anael, Chamuel	Venus
The Fool	Raphael, Uriel	Uranus
The Hanged Man	Asariel, Gabriel	Neptune
The Hermit	Raphael, Uriel	Virgo
The Heirophant	Anael, Sandalphon	Taurus
The High Priestess	Gabriel, Haniel	The Moon
Judgement	Azrael, Michael	Pluto
Justice	Anael, Jophiel	Libra
The Lovers	Anael, Raphael	Gemini
The Magician	Raphael, Raziel	Mercury
The Moon	Asariel, Sandalphon	Pisces
The Star	Anael, Uriel	Aquarius
Strength	Metatron, Michael	Leo
The Sun	Michael, Raphael	The Sun
Temperance	Sachiel, Zadkiel	Sagittarius
The Tower	Camael, Michael	Mars
The Wheel of Fortune	Sachiel, Zadkiel	Jupiter
The World	Cassiel, Uriel	Earth, Saturn

Your Birth Card

~Major Arcana~

 Aquarius - (Jan. 20 - Feb. 18)

 Leo - (July 23 - Aug. 22)

 Pisces - (Feb. 19 - March 20)

 Virgo - (Aug. 23 - Sept. 22)

 Aries - (March 21 - April 19)

 Libra - (Sept. 23 - Oct. 22)

 Taurus - (April 20 - May 20)

 Scorpio - (Oct. 23 - Nov. 21)

 Gemini - (May 21 - June 20)

 Sagittarius - (Nov. 22 - Dec. 21)

 Cancer - (June 21 - July 22)

 Capricorn - (Dec. 22 - Jan. 19)

Tarot Prompts/ Ideas

3 Card Spread

Past / Present / Future

Stop / Start / Continue

Action / Obstacle / Solution

Problem / Lesson / Advice

Opportunity / Challenge / Outcome

You / Path / Potential

You / Other Person / Relationship

2 Card Spread

Perception / Reality

Take action / Rest

Banish / Attract

Let it go / Keep it

Strength / Weakness

Mistake / Lesson

Emotion / Thought

Finances

What is blocking me from financial
success?

What steps do I need to take in order
to increase my financial wealth?

Is this the right time to invest
in a new project?

What are the advantages/disadvantages
if I buy or sell (ex. house)?

Relationships

What is causing a blockage
in my relationship?

What parts of myself do I need to work
on in order to have a balanced relationship?

What can I do in order to strengthen
my relationship with this person?

In what way have my relationships
made me stronger?

Health

What is my body trying to tell me?

What steps can I take to
achieve greater health?

What is the best way to support
my healing?

How can I reduce the stress in my life?

Spiritual

What truth am I hiding from myself?

What do my spirit guides want
me to know at this time?

What can I do to nurture my
spiritual growth?

Where am I expending energy that
could be better used elsewhere?

MONTH

_____

THE MONTH AHEAD

DATE -

CARDS -

DECK -

FOCUS -

    1 - SPIRITUAL FOCUS
    2 - WORLD FOCUS (HOME, JOB, ETC.)
    3 - THEME FOR THE MONTH
    4 - POSITIVE INFLUENCES
    5 - NEGATIVE INFLUENCES
    6 - DECK COMMENT
    7 - ADVICE

3

6

1   2

4   7

5

INTERPRETATION-

THE WEEK AHEAD

DATE -

CARDS -

DECK -

FOCUS -
1 - THEME FOR THE WEEK
2 - STRUGGLE/OBSTACLE
3 - SOMETHING TO BE GRATEFUL FOR
4 - THIS WEEK'S LESSON
5 - ADVICE

```
        [ 1 ]
[ 2 ]         [ 3 ]

    [ 4 ] [ 5 ]
```

INTERPRETATION-

_____
_____
_____
_____
_____
_____
_____
_____
_____
_____
_____
_____
_____
_____
_____
_____

DAILY DRAW

DATE -

CARD -

DECK -

KEYWORDS -

INTERPRETATION-

_____
_____
_____
_____
_____
_____
_____
_____

END OF DAY SUMMARY-

_____
_____
_____
_____
_____
_____
_____

DAILY DRAW

DATE -

CARD -

DECK -

KEYWORDS -

INTERPRETATION-

_____

_____

_____

_____

_____

_____

_____

_____

END OF DAY SUMMARY-

_____

_____

_____

_____

_____

_____

_____

DAILY DRAW

DATE -

CARD -

DECK -

KEYWORDS -

INTERPRETATION-

_____

_____

_____

_____

_____

_____

_____

_____

_____

END OF DAY SUMMARY-

_____

_____

_____

_____

_____

_____

_____

DAILY DRAW

DATE -

CARD -

DECK -

KEYWORDS -

INTERPRETATION-

_____
_____
_____
_____
_____
_____
_____
_____
_____

END OF DAY SUMMARY-

_____
_____
_____
_____
_____
_____
_____

DAILY DRAW

DATE -

CARD -

DECK -

KEYWORDS -

INTERPRETATION-

_____
_____
_____
_____
_____
_____
_____
_____

END OF DAY SUMMARY-

_____
_____
_____
_____
_____
_____
_____

DAILY DRAW

DATE -

CARD -

DECK -

KEYWORDS -

INTERPRETATION-

_____
_____
_____
_____
_____
_____
_____
_____

END OF DAY SUMMARY-

_____
_____
_____
_____
_____
_____

DAILY DRAW

DATE -

CARD -

DECK -

KEYWORDS -

INTERPRETATION-

_____
_____
_____
_____
_____
_____
_____
_____

END OF DAY SUMMARY-

_____
_____
_____
_____
_____
_____
_____
_____

THE WEEK AHEAD

DATE -

CARDS -

DECK -

FOCUS -
- 1 - THEME FOR THE WEEK
- 2 - STRUGGLE/OBSTACLE
- 3 - SOMETHING TO BE GRATEFUL FOR
- 4 - THIS WEEK'S LESSON
- 5 - ADVICE

```
        1
  2           3

     4    5
```

INTERPRETATION -

_____

_____

_____

_____

_____

_____

_____

_____

_____

_____

_____

_____

_____

_____

_____

_____

_____

_____

DAILY DRAW

DATE -

CARD -

DECK -

KEYWORDS -

INTERPRETATION-

_____
_____
_____
_____
_____
_____
_____
_____

END OF DAY SUMMARY-

_____
_____
_____
_____
_____
_____
_____

DAILY DRAW

DATE -

CARD -

DECK -

KEYWORDS -

INTERPRETATION-

_____
_____
_____
_____
_____
_____
_____
_____

END OF DAY SUMMARY-

_____
_____
_____
_____
_____
_____
_____

DAILY DRAW

DATE -

CARD -

DECK -

KEYWORDS -

INTERPRETATION-

_____
_____
_____
_____
_____
_____
_____

END OF DAY SUMMARY-

_____
_____
_____
_____
_____
_____
_____

DAILY DRAW

DATE -

CARD -

DECK -

KEYWORDS -

INTERPRETATION-

_____
_____
_____
_____
_____
_____
_____
_____
_____

END OF DAY SUMMARY-

_____
_____
_____
_____
_____
_____
_____

DAILY DRAW

DATE -

CARD -

DECK -

KEYWORDS -

INTERPRETATION-

_____
_____
_____
_____
_____
_____
_____
_____

END OF DAY SUMMARY-

_____
_____
_____
_____
_____
_____
_____
_____

DAILY DRAW

DATE -

CARD -

DECK -

KEYWORDS -

INTERPRETATION-

_____
_____
_____
_____
_____
_____
_____
_____
_____

END OF DAY SUMMARY-

_____
_____
_____
_____
_____
_____
_____

DAILY DRAW

DATE -

CARD -

DECK -

KEYWORDS -

INTERPRETATION-

_____
_____
_____
_____
_____
_____
_____
_____

END OF DAY SUMMARY-

_____
_____
_____
_____
_____
_____
_____

THE WEEK AHEAD

DATE -

CARDS -

DECK -

FOCUS -
1 - THEME FOR THE WEEK
2 - STRUGGLE/OBSTACLE
3 - SOMETHING TO BE GRATEFUL FOR
4 - THIS WEEK'S LESSON
5 - ADVICE

| 1 |
| 2 | 3 |
| 4 | 5 |

INTERPRETATION-

DAILY DRAW

DATE -

CARD -

DECK -

KEYWORDS -

INTERPRETATION-

_____
_____
_____
_____
_____
_____
_____
_____
_____

END OF DAY SUMMARY-

_____
_____
_____
_____
_____
_____
_____

DAILY DRAW

DATE -

CARD -

DECK -

KEYWORDS -

INTERPRETATION-

_____
_____
_____
_____
_____
_____
_____
_____

END OF DAY SUMMARY-

_____
_____
_____
_____
_____
_____
_____

DAILY DRAW

DATE -

CARD -

DECK -

KEYWORDS -

INTERPRETATION-

_____
_____
_____
_____
_____
_____
_____
_____

END OF DAY SUMMARY-

_____
_____
_____
_____
_____
_____
_____

DAILY DRAW

DATE -

CARD -

DECK -

KEYWORDS -

INTERPRETATION-

_____
_____
_____
_____
_____
_____
_____
_____

END OF DAY SUMMARY-

_____
_____
_____
_____
_____
_____
_____
_____

DAILY DRAW

DATE -

CARD -

DECK -

KEYWORDS -

INTERPRETATION-

_____
_____
_____
_____
_____
_____
_____
_____
_____

END OF DAY SUMMARY-

_____
_____
_____
_____
_____
_____
_____
_____

DAILY DRAW

DATE -

CARD -

DECK -

KEYWORDS -

INTERPRETATION-

_____
_____
_____
_____
_____
_____
_____
_____

END OF DAY SUMMARY-

_____
_____
_____
_____
_____
_____
_____

DAILY DRAW

DATE -

CARD -

DECK -

KEYWORDS -

INTERPRETATION-

_____
_____
_____
_____
_____
_____
_____
_____

END OF DAY SUMMARY-

_____
_____
_____
_____
_____
_____
_____

THE WEEK AHEAD

DATE -

CARDS -

DECK -

FOCUS -
   1 - THEME FOR THE WEEK
   2 - STRUGGLE/OBSTACLE
   3 - SOMETHING TO BE GRATEFUL FOR
   4 - THIS WEEK'S LESSON
   5 - ADVICE

```
           1
   2           3

      4    5
```

INTERPRETATION-

DAILY DRAW

DATE -

CARD -

DECK -

KEYWORDS -

INTERPRETATION-

_____
_____
_____
_____
_____
_____
_____
_____

END OF DAY SUMMARY-

_____
_____
_____
_____
_____
_____
_____

DAILY DRAW

DATE -

CARD -

DECK -

KEYWORDS -

INTERPRETATION-

_____
_____
_____
_____
_____
_____
_____
_____
_____
_____

END OF DAY SUMMARY-

_____
_____
_____
_____
_____
_____
_____
_____

DAILY DRAW

DATE -

CARD -

DECK -

KEYWORDS -

INTERPRETATION-

_____
_____
_____
_____
_____
_____
_____
_____
_____

END OF DAY SUMMARY-

_____
_____
_____
_____
_____
_____
_____
_____

DAILY DRAW

DATE -

CARD -

DECK -

KEYWORDS -

INTERPRETATION-

_____
_____
_____
_____
_____
_____
_____
_____

END OF DAY SUMMARY-

_____
_____
_____
_____
_____
_____
_____

DAILY DRAW

DATE -

CARD -

DECK -

KEYWORDS -

INTERPRETATION-

_____
_____
_____
_____
_____
_____
_____
_____

END OF DAY SUMMARY-

_____
_____
_____
_____
_____
_____
_____

DAILY DRAW

DATE -

CARD -

DECK -

KEYWORDS -

INTERPRETATION-

_____
_____
_____
_____
_____
_____
_____
_____
_____

END OF DAY SUMMARY-

_____
_____
_____
_____
_____
_____
_____
_____

DAILY DRAW

DATE -

CARD -

DECK -

KEYWORDS -

INTERPRETATION-

_____
_____
_____
_____
_____
_____
_____
_____

END OF DAY SUMMARY-

_____
_____
_____
_____
_____
_____
_____

A LOOK BACK

DATE -

USE THIS TIME TO LOOK BACK AT THE LAST MONTH, AND
REFLECT ON YOUR DRAWS. DID THE MESSAGES/ADVICE
RECEIVED RESONATE WITH YOU? WAS/IS ANYTHING
ABOUT YOUR READINGS UNCLEAR?

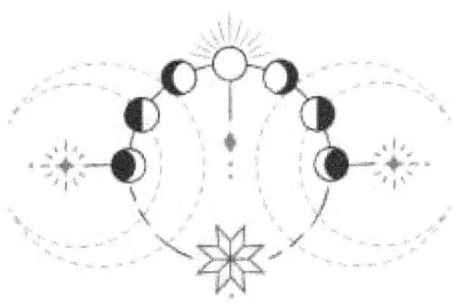

REFLECTIONS-

_____
_____
_____
_____
_____
_____
_____
_____
_____
_____
_____
_____
_____
_____
_____
_____
_____
_____

MONTH

_____

THE MONTH AHEAD

DATE -

CARDS -

DECK -

FOCUS -
    1 - SPIRITUAL FOCUS
    2 - WORLD FOCUS (HOME, JOB, ETC.)
    3 - THEME FOR THE MONTH
    4 - POSITIVE INFLUENCES
    5 - NEGATIVE INFLUENCES
    6 - DECK COMMENT
    7 - ADVICE

3

6

1

2

4

7

5

INTERPRETATION-

THE WEEK AHEAD

DATE -

CARDS -

DECK -

FOCUS -
    1 - THEME FOR THE WEEK
    2 - STRUGGLE/OBSTACLE
    3 - SOMETHING TO BE GRATEFUL FOR
    4 - THIS WEEK'S LESSON
    5 - ADVICE

	1	
2		3
	4	5

INTERPRETATION-

_____
_____
_____
_____
_____
_____
_____
_____
_____
_____
_____
_____
_____
_____
_____

DAILY DRAW

DATE -

CARD -

DECK -

KEYWORDS -

INTERPRETATION-

_____
_____
_____
_____
_____
_____
_____
_____

END OF DAY SUMMARY-

_____
_____
_____
_____
_____
_____
_____

DAILY DRAW

DATE -

CARD -

DECK -

KEYWORDS -

INTERPRETATION-

_____
_____
_____
_____
_____
_____
_____
_____

END OF DAY SUMMARY-

_____
_____
_____
_____
_____
_____
_____

DAILY DRAW

DATE -

CARD -

DECK -

KEYWORDS -

INTERPRETATION-

_____
_____
_____
_____
_____
_____
_____
_____
_____

END OF DAY SUMMARY-

_____
_____
_____
_____
_____
_____
_____

DAILY DRAW

DATE -

CARD -

DECK -

KEYWORDS -

INTERPRETATION-

_____
_____
_____
_____
_____
_____
_____
_____

END OF DAY SUMMARY-

_____
_____
_____
_____
_____
_____
_____

DAILY DRAW

DATE -

CARD -

DECK -

KEYWORDS -

INTERPRETATION-

_____
_____
_____
_____
_____
_____
_____
_____
_____

END OF DAY SUMMARY-

_____
_____
_____
_____
_____
_____

DAILY DRAW

DATE -

CARD -

DECK -

KEYWORDS -

INTERPRETATION-

_____
_____
_____
_____
_____
_____
_____
_____

END OF DAY SUMMARY-

_____
_____
_____
_____
_____
_____
_____

DAILY DRAW

DATE -

CARD -

DECK -

KEYWORDS -

INTERPRETATION-

_____
_____
_____
_____
_____
_____
_____
_____

END OF DAY SUMMARY-

_____
_____
_____
_____
_____
_____
_____

THE WEEK AHEAD

DATE -

CARDS -

DECK -

FOCUS -
- 1 - THEME FOR THE WEEK
- 2 - STRUGGLE/OBSTACLE
- 3 - SOMETHING TO BE GRATEFUL FOR
- 4 - THIS WEEK'S LESSON
- 5 - ADVICE

```
        1
   2         3

     4    5
```

INTERPRETATION-

_____
_____
_____
_____
_____
_____
_____
_____
_____
_____
_____
_____
_____
_____
_____
_____
_____

DAILY DRAW

DATE -

CARD -

DECK -

KEYWORDS -

INTERPRETATION-

_____

_____

_____

_____

_____

_____

_____

_____

END OF DAY SUMMARY-

_____

_____

_____

_____

_____

_____

DAILY DRAW

DATE -

CARD -

DECK -

KEYWORDS -

INTERPRETATION-

_____
_____
_____
_____
_____
_____
_____
_____
_____

END OF DAY SUMMARY-

_____
_____
_____
_____
_____
_____
_____

DAILY DRAW

DATE -

CARD -

DECK -

KEYWORDS -

INTERPRETATION-

_____
_____
_____
_____
_____
_____
_____
_____

END OF DAY SUMMARY-

_____
_____
_____
_____
_____
_____
_____

DAILY DRAW

DATE -

CARD -

DECK -

KEYWORDS -

INTERPRETATION-

_____
_____
_____
_____
_____
_____
_____
_____

END OF DAY SUMMARY-

_____
_____
_____
_____
_____
_____
_____

DAILY DRAW

DATE -

CARD -

DECK -

KEYWORDS -

INTERPRETATION-

_____
_____
_____
_____
_____
_____
_____
_____

END OF DAY SUMMARY-

_____
_____
_____
_____
_____
_____

DAILY DRAW

DATE -

CARD -

DECK -

KEYWORDS -

INTERPRETATION-

_____
_____
_____
_____
_____
_____
_____
_____

END OF DAY SUMMARY-

_____
_____
_____
_____
_____
_____
_____

DAILY DRAW

DATE -

CARD -

DECK -

KEYWORDS -

INTERPRETATION-

_____
_____
_____
_____
_____
_____
_____
_____
_____

END OF DAY SUMMARY-

_____
_____
_____
_____
_____
_____
_____
_____

THE WEEK AHEAD

DATE -

CARDS -

DECK -

FOCUS -
    1 - THEME FOR THE WEEK
    2 - STRUGGLE/OBSTACLE
    3 - SOMETHING TO BE GRATEFUL FOR
    4 - THIS WEEK'S LESSON
    5 - ADVICE

1

2   **3**

4   **5**

INTERPRETATION-

_____
_____
_____
_____
_____
_____
_____
_____
_____
_____
_____
_____
_____
_____
_____
_____
_____
_____
_____

DAILY DRAW

DATE -

CARD -

DECK -

KEYWORDS -

INTERPRETATION-

_____
_____
_____
_____
_____
_____
_____
_____

END OF DAY SUMMARY-

_____
_____
_____
_____
_____
_____

DAILY DRAW

DATE -

CARD -

DECK -

KEYWORDS -

INTERPRETATION-

_____
_____
_____
_____
_____
_____
_____
_____

END OF DAY SUMMARY-

_____
_____
_____
_____
_____
_____
_____

DAILY DRAW

DATE -

CARD -

DECK -

KEYWORDS -

INTERPRETATION-

_____
_____
_____
_____
_____
_____
_____
_____

END OF DAY SUMMARY-

_____
_____
_____
_____
_____
_____
_____

DAILY DRAW

DATE -

CARD -

DECK -

KEYWORDS -

INTERPRETATION-

_____
_____
_____
_____
_____
_____
_____
_____
_____

END OF DAY SUMMARY-

_____
_____
_____
_____
_____
_____
_____
_____

DAILY DRAW

DATE -

CARD -

DECK -

KEYWORDS -

INTERPRETATION-

_____
_____
_____
_____
_____
_____
_____
_____

END OF DAY SUMMARY-

_____
_____
_____
_____
_____
_____
_____

DAILY DRAW

DATE -

CARD -

DECK -

KEYWORDS -

INTERPRETATION-

_____
_____
_____
_____
_____
_____
_____

END OF DAY SUMMARY-

_____
_____
_____
_____
_____
_____

DAILY DRAW

DATE -

CARD -

DECK -

KEYWORDS -

INTERPRETATION-

_____
_____
_____
_____
_____
_____
_____
_____

END OF DAY SUMMARY-

_____
_____
_____
_____
_____
_____
_____

THE WEEK AHEAD

DATE -

CARDS -

DECK -

FOCUS -
    1 - THEME FOR THE WEEK
    2 - STRUGGLE/OBSTACLE
    3 - SOMETHING TO BE GRATEFUL FOR
    4 - THIS WEEK'S LESSON
    5 - ADVICE

```
        1
  2          3

     4    5
```

INTERPRETATION-

_____
_____
_____
_____
_____
_____
_____
_____
_____
_____
_____
_____
_____
_____
_____
_____

DAILY DRAW

DATE -

CARD -

DECK -

KEYWORDS -

INTERPRETATION-

_____

_____

_____

_____

_____

_____

_____

_____

END OF DAY SUMMARY-

_____

_____

_____

_____

_____

_____

_____

DAILY DRAW

DATE -

CARD -

DECK -

KEYWORDS -

INTERPRETATION-

_____
_____
_____
_____
_____
_____
_____
_____
_____

END OF DAY SUMMARY-

_____
_____
_____
_____
_____
_____
_____

DAILY DRAW

DATE -

CARD -

DECK -

KEYWORDS -

INTERPRETATION-

_____
_____
_____
_____
_____
_____
_____
_____

END OF DAY SUMMARY-

_____
_____
_____
_____
_____
_____

DAILY DRAW

DATE -

CARD -

DECK -

KEYWORDS -

INTERPRETATION-

_____
_____
_____
_____
_____
_____
_____
_____

END OF DAY SUMMARY-

_____
_____
_____
_____
_____
_____
_____

DAILY DRAW

DATE -

CARD -

DECK -

KEYWORDS -

INTERPRETATION-

_____
_____
_____
_____
_____
_____
_____
_____

END OF DAY SUMMARY-

_____
_____
_____
_____
_____
_____
_____

DAILY DRAW

DATE -

CARD -

DECK -

KEYWORDS -

INTERPRETATION-

_____
_____
_____
_____
_____
_____
_____
_____

END OF DAY SUMMARY-

_____
_____
_____
_____
_____
_____
_____

DAILY DRAW

DATE -

CARD -

DECK -

KEYWORDS -

INTERPRETATION-

_____
_____
_____
_____
_____
_____
_____
_____
_____

END OF DAY SUMMARY-

_____
_____
_____
_____
_____
_____
_____

A LOOK BACK

DATE -

USE THIS TIME TO LOOK BACK AT THE LAST MONTH, AND
REFLECT ON YOUR DRAWS. DID THE MESSAGES/ADVICE
RECEIVED RESONATE WITH YOU? WAS/IS ANYTHING
ABOUT YOUR READINGS UNCLEAR?

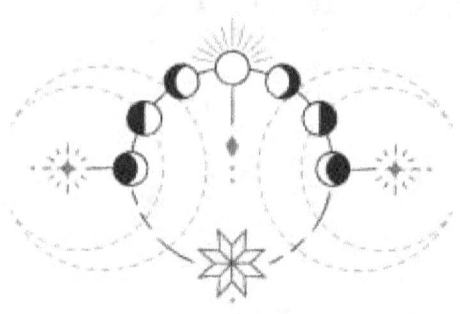

REFLECTIONS-

_____
_____
_____
_____
_____
_____
_____
_____
_____
_____
_____
_____
_____
_____
_____
_____
_____
_____

MONTH

_____

THE MONTH AHEAD

DATE -

CARDS -

```
        3
              6
   1    2
```

DECK -

FOCUS -
- 1 - SPIRITUAL FOCUS
- 2 - WORLD FOCUS (HOME, JOB, ETC.)
- 3 - THEME FOR THE MONTH
- 4 - POSITIVE INFLUENCES
- 5 - NEGATIVE INFLUENCES
- 6 - DECK COMMENT
- 7 - ADVICE

```
        4
              7

        5
```

INTERPRETATION-

_____
_____
_____
_____
_____
_____
_____
_____
_____
_____
_____
_____
_____
_____
_____
_____
_____
_____

THE WEEK AHEAD

DATE -

CARDS -

DECK -

FOCUS -
   1 - THEME FOR THE WEEK
   2 - STRUGGLE/OBSTACLE
   3 - SOMETHING TO BE GRATEFUL FOR
   4 - THIS WEEK'S LESSON
   5 - ADVICE

```
          1
   2          3

      4     5
```

INTERPRETATION-

_____
_____
_____
_____
_____
_____
_____
_____
_____
_____
_____
_____
_____
_____
_____
_____
_____

DAILY DRAW

DATE -

CARD -

DECK -

KEYWORDS -

INTERPRETATION-

_____
_____
_____
_____
_____
_____
_____
_____

END OF DAY SUMMARY-

_____
_____
_____
_____
_____
_____
_____

DAILY DRAW

DATE -

CARD -

DECK -

KEYWORDS -

INTERPRETATION-

_____
_____
_____
_____
_____
_____
_____
_____

END OF DAY SUMMARY-

_____
_____
_____
_____
_____
_____
_____

DAILY DRAW

DATE -

CARD -

DECK -

KEYWORDS -

INTERPRETATION-

_____
_____
_____
_____
_____
_____
_____
_____

END OF DAY SUMMARY-

_____
_____
_____
_____
_____
_____
_____

DAILY DRAW

DATE -

CARD -

DECK -

KEYWORDS -

INTERPRETATION-

_____
_____
_____
_____
_____
_____
_____
_____

END OF DAY SUMMARY-

_____
_____
_____
_____
_____
_____
_____
_____

DAILY DRAW

DATE -

CARD -

DECK -

KEYWORDS -

INTERPRETATION-

_____

_____

_____

_____

_____

_____

_____

_____

END OF DAY SUMMARY-

_____

_____

_____

_____

_____

_____

_____

DAILY DRAW

DATE -

CARD -

DECK -

KEYWORDS -

INTERPRETATION-

_____
_____
_____
_____
_____
_____
_____
_____

END OF DAY SUMMARY-

_____
_____
_____
_____
_____
_____
_____

DAILY DRAW

DATE -

CARD -

DECK -

KEYWORDS -

INTERPRETATION-

_____
_____
_____
_____
_____
_____
_____
_____

END OF DAY SUMMARY-

_____
_____
_____
_____
_____
_____
_____

THE WEEK AHEAD

DATE -

CARDS -

DECK -

FOCUS -
1 - THEME FOR THE WEEK
2 - STRUGGLE/OBSTACLE
3 - SOMETHING TO BE GRATEFUL FOR
4 - THIS WEEK'S LESSON
5 - ADVICE

```
        1
  2         3

     4   5
```

INTERPRETATION-

_____
_____
_____
_____
_____
_____
_____
_____
_____
_____
_____
_____
_____
_____
_____
_____

DAILY DRAW

DATE -

CARD -

DECK -

KEYWORDS -

INTERPRETATION-

_____
_____
_____
_____
_____
_____
_____
_____

END OF DAY SUMMARY-

_____
_____
_____
_____
_____
_____
_____
_____

DAILY DRAW

DATE -

CARD -

DECK -

KEYWORDS -

INTERPRETATION-

_____
_____
_____
_____
_____
_____
_____
_____
_____

END OF DAY SUMMARY-

_____
_____
_____
_____
_____
_____
_____

DAILY DRAW

DATE -

CARD -

DECK -

KEYWORDS -

INTERPRETATION-

_____
_____
_____
_____
_____
_____
_____
_____

END OF DAY SUMMARY-

_____
_____
_____
_____
_____
_____
_____

DAILY DRAW

DATE -

CARD -

DECK -

KEYWORDS -

INTERPRETATION-

_____
_____
_____
_____
_____
_____
_____
_____

END OF DAY SUMMARY-

_____
_____
_____
_____
_____
_____
_____

DAILY DRAW

DATE -

CARD -

DECK -

KEYWORDS -

INTERPRETATION-

_____
_____
_____
_____
_____
_____
_____
_____

END OF DAY SUMMARY-

_____
_____
_____
_____
_____
_____
_____
_____

DAILY DRAW

DATE -

CARD -

DECK -

KEYWORDS -

INTERPRETATION-

_____
_____
_____
_____
_____
_____
_____
_____

END OF DAY SUMMARY-

_____
_____
_____
_____
_____
_____
_____

DAILY DRAW

DATE -

CARD -

DECK -

KEYWORDS -

INTERPRETATION-

_____
_____
_____
_____
_____
_____
_____
_____

END OF DAY SUMMARY-

_____
_____
_____
_____
_____
_____
_____

THE WEEK AHEAD

DATE -

CARDS -

DECK -

FOCUS -
    1 - THEME FOR THE WEEK
    2 - STRUGGLE/OBSTACLE
    3 - SOMETHING TO BE GRATEFUL FOR
    4 - THIS WEEK'S LESSON
    5 - ADVICE

	1	
2		3
	4	5

INTERPRETATION-

_____
_____
_____
_____
_____
_____
_____
_____
_____
_____
_____
_____
_____
_____
_____
_____

DAILY DRAW

DATE -

CARD -

DECK -

KEYWORDS -

INTERPRETATION-

_____
_____
_____
_____
_____
_____
_____
_____

END OF DAY SUMMARY-

_____
_____
_____
_____
_____
_____
_____

DAILY DRAW

DATE -

CARD -

DECK -

KEYWORDS -

INTERPRETATION-

_____
_____
_____
_____
_____
_____
_____
_____

END OF DAY SUMMARY-

_____
_____
_____
_____
_____
_____
_____

DAILY DRAW

DATE -

CARD -

DECK -

KEYWORDS -

INTERPRETATION-

_____
_____
_____
_____
_____
_____
_____
_____

END OF DAY SUMMARY-

_____
_____
_____
_____
_____
_____
_____

DAILY DRAW

DATE -

CARD -

DECK -

KEYWORDS -

INTERPRETATION-

_____
_____
_____
_____
_____
_____
_____
_____

END OF DAY SUMMARY-

_____
_____
_____
_____
_____
_____
_____

DAILY DRAW

DATE -

CARD -

DECK -

KEYWORDS -

INTERPRETATION-

_____
_____
_____
_____
_____
_____
_____
_____

END OF DAY SUMMARY-

_____
_____
_____
_____
_____
_____
_____
_____

DAILY DRAW

DATE -

CARD -

DECK -

KEYWORDS -

INTERPRETATION-

_____
_____
_____
_____
_____
_____
_____
_____
_____

END OF DAY SUMMARY-

_____
_____
_____
_____
_____
_____
_____

DAILY DRAW

DATE -

CARD -

DECK -

KEYWORDS -

INTERPRETATION-

_____
_____
_____
_____
_____
_____
_____
_____
_____

END OF DAY SUMMARY-

_____
_____
_____
_____
_____
_____
_____
_____

THE WEEK AHEAD

DATE -

CARDS -

DECK -

FOCUS -
1 - THEME FOR THE WEEK
2 - STRUGGLE/OBSTACLE
3 - SOMETHING TO BE GRATEFUL FOR
4 - THIS WEEK'S LESSON
5 - ADVICE

	1	
2		3
	4	5

INTERPRETATION-

DAILY DRAW

DATE -

CARD -

DECK -

KEYWORDS -

INTERPRETATION-

_____
_____
_____
_____
_____
_____
_____
_____

END OF DAY SUMMARY-

_____
_____
_____
_____
_____
_____
_____

DAILY DRAW

DATE -

CARD -

DECK -

KEYWORDS -

INTERPRETATION-

_____
_____
_____
_____
_____
_____
_____
_____

END OF DAY SUMMARY-

_____
_____
_____
_____
_____
_____
_____

DAILY DRAW

DATE -

CARD -

DECK -

KEYWORDS -

INTERPRETATION-

_____
_____
_____
_____
_____
_____
_____
_____

END OF DAY SUMMARY-

_____
_____
_____
_____
_____
_____
_____

DAILY DRAW

DATE -

CARD -

DECK -

KEYWORDS -

INTERPRETATION-

_____

_____

_____

_____

_____

_____

_____

_____

_____

END OF DAY SUMMARY-

_____

_____

_____

_____

_____

_____

DAILY DRAW

DATE -

CARD -

DECK -

KEYWORDS -

INTERPRETATION-

_____
_____
_____
_____
_____
_____
_____
_____
_____

END OF DAY SUMMARY-

_____
_____
_____
_____
_____
_____
_____

DAILY DRAW

DATE -

CARD -

DECK -

KEYWORDS -

INTERPRETATION-

_____
_____
_____
_____
_____
_____
_____
_____

END OF DAY SUMMARY-

_____
_____
_____
_____
_____
_____
_____

DAILY DRAW

DATE -

CARD -

DECK -

KEYWORDS -

INTERPRETATION-

_____
_____
_____
_____
_____
_____
_____
_____
_____

END OF DAY SUMMARY-

_____
_____
_____
_____
_____
_____
_____
_____

A LOOK BACK

DATE -

USE THIS TIME TO LOOK BACK AT THE LAST MONTH, AND
REFLECT ON YOUR DRAWS. DID THE MESSAGES/ADVICE
RECEIVED RESONATE WITH YOU? WAS/IS ANYTHING
ABOUT YOUR READINGS UNCLEAR?

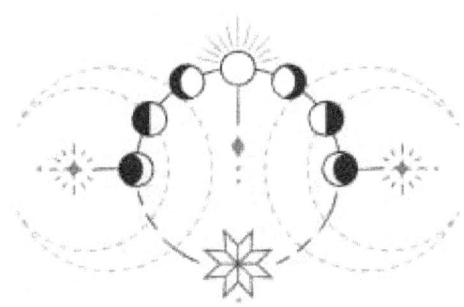

REFLECTIONS-

_____
_____
_____
_____
_____
_____
_____
_____
_____
_____
_____
_____
_____
_____
_____
_____
_____
_____
_____
_____
_____

MONTH

_____

THE MONTH AHEAD

DATE -

CARDS -

3

6

1   2

DECK -

FOCUS -
  1 - SPIRITUAL FOCUS
  2 - WORLD FOCUS (HOME, JOB, ETC.)
  3 - THEME FOR THE MONTH
  4 - POSITIVE INFLUENCES
  5 - NEGATIVE INFLUENCES
  6 - DECK COMMENT
  7 - ADVICE

4

7

5

INTERPRETATION-

_____

_____

_____

_____

_____

_____

_____

_____

_____

_____

_____

_____

_____

_____

_____

_____

_____

_____

_____

_____

THE WEEK AHEAD

DATE -

CARDS -

DECK -

FOCUS -
  1 - THEME FOR THE WEEK
  2 - STRUGGLE/OBSTACLE
  3 - SOMETHING TO BE GRATEFUL FOR
  4 - THIS WEEK'S LESSON
  5 - ADVICE

1

2

3

4

5

INTERPRETATION-

DAILY DRAW

DATE -

CARD -

DECK -

KEYWORDS -

INTERPRETATION-

_____
_____
_____
_____
_____
_____
_____
_____
_____

END OF DAY SUMMARY-

_____
_____
_____
_____
_____
_____
_____

DAILY DRAW

DATE -

CARD -

DECK -

KEYWORDS -

INTERPRETATION-

_____
_____
_____
_____
_____
_____
_____
_____

END OF DAY SUMMARY-

_____
_____
_____
_____
_____
_____
_____

DAILY DRAW

DATE -

CARD -

DECK -

KEYWORDS -

INTERPRETATION-

_____
_____
_____
_____
_____
_____
_____
_____

END OF DAY SUMMARY-

_____
_____
_____
_____
_____
_____
_____

DAILY DRAW

DATE -

CARD -

DECK -

KEYWORDS -

INTERPRETATION-

_____
_____
_____
_____
_____
_____
_____
_____

END OF DAY SUMMARY-

_____
_____
_____
_____
_____
_____
_____

DAILY DRAW

DATE -

CARD -

DECK -

KEYWORDS -

INTERPRETATION-

_____
_____
_____
_____
_____
_____
_____
_____

END OF DAY SUMMARY-

_____
_____
_____
_____
_____
_____
_____

DAILY DRAW

DATE -

CARD -

DECK -

KEYWORDS -

INTERPRETATION-

_____
_____
_____
_____
_____
_____
_____
_____

END OF DAY SUMMARY-

_____
_____
_____
_____
_____
_____
_____
_____

DAILY DRAW

DATE -

CARD -

DECK -

KEYWORDS -

INTERPRETATION-

_____
_____
_____
_____
_____
_____
_____
_____
_____

END OF DAY SUMMARY-

_____
_____
_____
_____
_____
_____

THE WEEK AHEAD

DATE -

CARDS -

DECK -

FOCUS -
1 - THEME FOR THE WEEK
2 - STRUGGLE/OBSTACLE
3 - SOMETHING TO BE GRATEFUL FOR
4 - THIS WEEK'S LESSON
5 - ADVICE

1

2   **3**

4   **5**

INTERPRETATION-

DAILY DRAW

DATE -

CARD -

DECK -

KEYWORDS -

INTERPRETATION-

_____
_____
_____
_____
_____
_____
_____
_____

END OF DAY SUMMARY-

_____
_____
_____
_____
_____
_____
_____

DAILY DRAW

DATE -

CARD -

DECK -

KEYWORDS -

INTERPRETATION-

_____
_____
_____
_____
_____
_____
_____
_____

END OF DAY SUMMARY-

_____
_____
_____
_____
_____
_____
_____

DAILY DRAW

DATE -

CARD -

DECK -

KEYWORDS -

INTERPRETATION-

_____
_____
_____
_____
_____
_____
_____
_____
_____

END OF DAY SUMMARY-

_____
_____
_____
_____
_____
_____
_____

DAILY DRAW

DATE -

CARD -

DECK -

KEYWORDS -

INTERPRETATION-

_____
_____
_____
_____
_____
_____
_____
_____

END OF DAY SUMMARY-

_____
_____
_____
_____
_____
_____
_____

DAILY DRAW

DATE -

CARD -

DECK -

KEYWORDS -

INTERPRETATION-

_____
_____
_____
_____
_____
_____
_____
_____
_____

END OF DAY SUMMARY-

_____
_____
_____
_____
_____
_____
_____
_____

DAILY DRAW

DATE -

CARD -

DECK -

KEYWORDS -

INTERPRETATION-

_____
_____
_____
_____
_____
_____
_____
_____
_____

END OF DAY SUMMARY-

_____
_____
_____
_____
_____
_____
_____

DAILY DRAW

DATE -

CARD -

DECK -

KEYWORDS -

INTERPRETATION-

_____
_____
_____
_____
_____
_____
_____
_____

END OF DAY SUMMARY-

_____
_____
_____
_____
_____
_____
_____

THE WEEK AHEAD

DATE -

CARDS -

DECK -

FOCUS -
    1 - THEME FOR THE WEEK
    2 - STRUGGLE/OBSTACLE
    3 - SOMETHING TO BE GRATEFUL FOR
    4 - THIS WEEK'S LESSON
    5 - ADVICE

	1	
2		3
	4	5

INTERPRETATION-

DAILY DRAW

DATE -

CARD -

DECK -

KEYWORDS -

INTERPRETATION-

_____
_____
_____
_____
_____
_____
_____
_____
_____

END OF DAY SUMMARY-

_____
_____
_____
_____
_____
_____
_____
_____

DAILY DRAW

DATE -

CARD -

DECK -

KEYWORDS -

INTERPRETATION-

_____
_____
_____
_____
_____
_____
_____
_____

END OF DAY SUMMARY-

_____
_____
_____
_____
_____
_____
_____
_____

DAILY DRAW

DATE -

CARD -

DECK -

KEYWORDS -

INTERPRETATION-

_____
_____
_____
_____
_____
_____
_____
_____
_____

END OF DAY SUMMARY-

_____
_____
_____
_____
_____
_____
_____

DAILY DRAW

DATE -

CARD -

DECK -

KEYWORDS -

INTERPRETATION-

_____
_____
_____
_____
_____
_____
_____
_____

END OF DAY SUMMARY-

_____
_____
_____
_____
_____
_____
_____
_____

DAILY DRAW

DATE -

CARD -

DECK -

KEYWORDS -

INTERPRETATION-

_____
_____
_____
_____
_____
_____
_____
_____

END OF DAY SUMMARY-

_____
_____
_____
_____
_____
_____
_____

DAILY DRAW

DATE -

CARD -

DECK -

KEYWORDS -

INTERPRETATION-

_____
_____
_____
_____
_____
_____
_____
_____
_____

END OF DAY SUMMARY-

_____
_____
_____
_____
_____
_____
_____

DAILY DRAW

DATE -

CARD -

DECH -

KEYWORDS -

INTERPRETATION-

_____
_____
_____
_____
_____
_____
_____
_____

END OF DAY SUMMARY-

_____
_____
_____
_____
_____
_____
_____

THE WEEK AHEAD

DATE -

CARDS -

DECK -

FOCUS -
    1 - THEME FOR THE WEEK
    2 - STRUGGLE/OBSTACLE
    3 - SOMETHING TO BE GRATEFUL FOR
    4 - THIS WEEK'S LESSON
    5 - ADVICE

	1	
2		3
4	5	

INTERPRETATION-

_____
_____
_____
_____
_____
_____
_____
_____
_____
_____
_____
_____
_____
_____
_____
_____
_____
_____

DAILY DRAW

DATE -

CARD -

DECK -

KEYWORDS -

INTERPRETATION-

_____
_____
_____
_____
_____
_____
_____
_____

END OF DAY SUMMARY-

_____
_____
_____
_____
_____
_____

DAILY DRAW

DATE -

CARD -

DECK -

KEYWORDS -

INTERPRETATION-

_____
_____
_____
_____
_____
_____
_____
_____

END OF DAY SUMMARY-

_____
_____
_____
_____
_____
_____
_____
_____

DAILY DRAW

DATE -

CARD -

DECK -

KEYWORDS -

INTERPRETATION-

_____
_____
_____
_____
_____
_____
_____
_____

END OF DAY SUMMARY-

_____
_____
_____
_____
_____
_____
_____

DAILY DRAW

DATE -

CARD -

DECK -

KEYWORDS -

INTERPRETATION-

_____
_____
_____
_____
_____
_____
_____
_____

END OF DAY SUMMARY-

_____
_____
_____
_____
_____
_____
_____

DAILY DRAW

DATE -

CARD -

DECK -

KEYWORDS -

INTERPRETATION-

_____
_____
_____
_____
_____
_____
_____
_____

END OF DAY SUMMARY-

_____
_____
_____
_____
_____
_____
_____

DAILY DRAW

DATE -

CARD -

DECK -

KEYWORDS -

INTERPRETATION-

_____
_____
_____
_____
_____
_____
_____
_____

END OF DAY SUMMARY-

_____
_____
_____
_____
_____
_____
_____
_____

DAILY DRAW

DATE -

CARD -

DECK -

KEYWORDS -

INTERPRETATION-

_____
_____
_____
_____
_____
_____
_____
_____

END OF DAY SUMMARY-

_____
_____
_____
_____
_____
_____
_____

A LOOK BACK

DATE -

USE THIS TIME TO LOOK BACK AT THE LAST MONTH, AND
REFLECT ON YOUR DRAWS. DID THE MESSAGES/ADVICE
RECEIVED RESONATE WITH YOU? WAS/IS ANYTHING
ABOUT YOUR READINGS UNCLEAR?

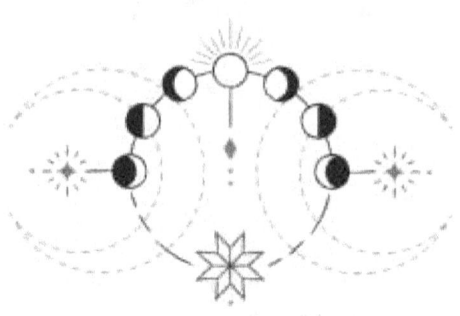

REFLECTIONS-

_____
_____
_____
_____
_____
_____
_____
_____
_____
_____
_____
_____
_____
_____
_____
_____
_____
_____

Creating Your Own
Tarot Spread

1. The Layout - The shape, or lack of, is totally dependent on you. If you're reading for someone else though, you may want to consider making it visually attractive. Some of the sacred geometry shapes are circle, square, pyramid, heart, and cross. But there's nothing wrong with laying your cards out in a row if you so choose.

2. Identify the specific question that needs to be addressed.

3. Create your spread so that it will lead you to the answer.

4. Yes or No questions are fine, but shouldn't be used for each card as you may need more elaboration regarding the specific question.

YOU ARE

XVII

THE STAR

www.ingramcontent.com/pod-product-compliance
Lightning Source LLC
Chambersburg PA
CBHW070709130626
46553CB00005B/1911